W9-AYO-171

Man

A BLUE BANNER
BIOGRAPHY

Peyton Manning

Joanne Mattern

P.O. Box 196
Hockessin, Delaware 19707
Visit us on the web: www.mitchelllane.com
Comments? email us: mitchelllane@mitchelllane.com

Mitchell Lane PUBLISHERS

Printing		2	3	4	5	6	7	8	9

Blue Banner Biographies

Alicia Keys	Allen Iverson	Alan Jackson
Ashanti	Ashlee Simpson	Ashton Kutcher
Avril Lavigne	Beyoncé	Bow Wow
Britney Spears	Christina Aguilera	Christopher Paul Curtis
Clay Aiken	Condoleezza Rice	Daniel Radcliffe
Derek Jeter	Eminem	Eve
50-Cent	Gwen Stefani	Ice Cube
Jamie Foxx	Ja Rule	Jay-Z
Jennifer Lopez	J. K. Rowling	Jodie Foster
Justin Berfield	Kate Hudson	Kelly Clarkson
Kenny Chesney	Lance Armstrong	Lindsay Lohan
Mariah Carey	Mario	Mary-Kate and Ashley Olsen
Melissa Gilbert	Michael Jackson	Miguel Tejada
Missy Elliott	Nelly	Orlando Bloom
Paris Hilton	P. Diddy	**Peyton Manning**
Queen Latifah	Rita Williams-Garcia	Ritchie Valens
Ron Howard	Rudy Giuliani	Sally Field
Selena	Shirley Temple	Tim McGraw
Usher		

Library of Congress Cataloging-in-Publication Data
Mattern, Joanne, 1963–
    Peyton Manning / by Joanne Mattern
        p. cm. — (Blue banner biographies)
    Includes bibliographical references and index.
    ISBN 1-58415-506-X (lib. bdg. : alk. paper)
    1. Manning, Peyton—Juvenile literature. 2. Football players—United States—Biography—Juvenile literature. I. Title. II. Blue banner biography.
GV939.M29M28 2006
796.332092—dc22
                                                                                            2005036692

ISBN-10: 1-58415-506-X

ISBN-13: 978-1-58415-506-5

ABOUT THE AUTHOR: Joanne Mattern is the author of more than 200 nonfiction books for children, including *Brian McBride* and *Miguel Tejada* for Mitchell Lane Publishers. Along with biographies, she has written extensively about animals, nature, history, sports, and foreign cultures. She lives near New York City with her husband and three young daughters.

CONTENTS

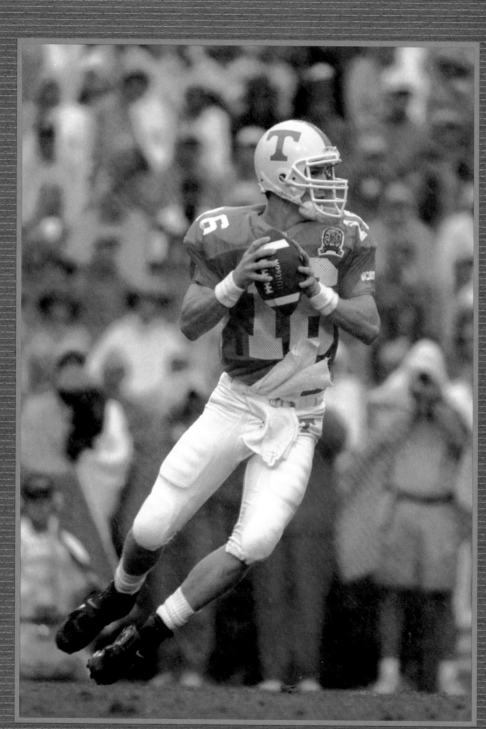

In college, Peyton Manning was an outstanding quarterback for the University of Tennessee Volunteers.

A Tough Decision

*P*eyton Manning did not know what to do. He had been a student at the University of Tennessee for three years. He was the star quarterback of the university's football team. With Peyton's help, the University of Tennessee Volunteers had become a terrific team. Peyton was a great player.

Peyton was so good that many teams in the National Football League (NFL) wanted him to play for them. Peyton wanted to play in the NFL too. His father, Archie Manning, had been a professional football player. Peyton always dreamed of following in his father's footsteps.

Almost everyone told Peyton that leaving school was a good idea. Even though he was only a junior, he had taken enough classes to graduate. He could make a lot of money in the NFL.

However, Peyton thought staying in school seemed like a good idea too. He loved playing for the Volunteers. He had many friends at school. Also, people at the school were counting on Peyton to stay.

Quarterback Peyton Manning calls the snap count during the Tennessee Volunteers' 30-24 victory over the UCLA Bruins.

Peyton thought a lot. He talked to coaches. He talked to other players. He talked to his family. Then he made up his mind.

On March 5, 1997, Peyton called a press conference. As he walked up to the microphone, people in the audience held their breath. Would Peyton stay? Would he leave?

"I made up my mind and I don't expect to ever look back," Peyton said. "I am going to stay at the University of Tennessee."

The room burst into cheers. Peyton had made a tough choice, but he knew he had done the right thing. The young quarterback had made other tough decisions in his life. He always took the time to think things over. He always talked to his family.

Peyton's background and his careful thinking made him a success on the football field. They have made him a success in life as well.

"I made up my mind and I don't expect to ever look back," Peyton said. "I am going to stay at the University of Tennessee."

Football Family

Peyton Williams Manning was born on March 24, 1976. He is the second son of Archie and Olivia Manning. Peyton has a brother named Cooper. Cooper is two years older than Peyton. Later, the Mannings would have another son. Elisha Nelson, called Eli, was born four years after Peyton.

Peyton was born in New Orleans, Louisiana. The Mannings lived in New Orleans because Archie Manning was the quarterback for the NFL's New Orleans Saints. Before he joined the Saints, Archie was a star quarterback at the University of Mississippi. That school is called Ole Miss. Many people think Archie Manning was the best football player Ole Miss ever had.

When Peyton and his brothers were growing up, football was the center of their lives. Every Christmas, the boys received new balls, jerseys, and other football equipment. The yard of their big yellow house became a favorite place to toss the football around.

Sundays were a special day for the Manning family. That was the day when Archie Manning and the Saints played

Peyton's father, Archie Manning, was the star quarterback for the New Orleans Saints during the 1970s and 1980s.

football. Peyton, his mother, and his brothers always went to the games.

Archie Manning was a great quarterback. However, the Saints were not a very good team. During the eleven years Archie played for them, they never had a winning season. They never made it to the playoffs. Still, Peyton and his brothers loved to cheer for them.

Football was important to the Mannings. However, Peyton's parents made sure the boys knew it wasn't the only thing in life.

After each game, the Manning boys got a special treat. They were allowed to visit the locker room. Even more fun, they were allowed to play on the field of the Louisiana Superdome. Peyton and Cooper loved to pretend they were NFL stars. Usually, Cooper ended up tackling Peyton. Then Peyton would get mad and cry. "He was kind of a baby," Olivia Manning once said about her son. Archie Manning got used to breaking up the many fights between the brothers.

Football was important to the Mannings. However, Peyton's parents made sure the boys knew it wasn't the only thing in life. "Football was never the most important thing in raising our children," Olivia Manning said. She and Archie worked hard to instill strong values in their sons. They made sure the boys were respectful. They raised Peyton and his brothers to care about others. Peyton's parents said the four most important things in life were religious faith, family, education, and athletics, in that order.

Archie Manning set a good example of how a star player should behave. "There were a lot of days when he got beat up on the field and the Saints lost badly," Peyton once said. "But he signed every autograph, he did every single interview, and that's what it's all about." Archie also displayed good sportsmanship. He never spoke badly about another player. Peyton and his brothers grew up with those same strong values.

Although the Manning boys loved to play football, their father thought the sport was too rough for little boys to play. He wanted the boys to wait until they were older before they joined their school or local teams. "When you are a kid, you do sports for fun, period," Archie later wrote.

Still, it was impossible to keep the Manning boys away from football. Cooper was the quarterback of his school team in fifth grade. Peyton followed right behind him. The boys attended a private school called the Isidore Newman School from kindergarten through twelfth grade. The school's football team was well known.

In 1991, Peyton was a sophomore at Isidore Newman. He was also the school's starting quarterback. Cooper was a senior and also on the team. He was a wide receiver. The brothers made up secret hand signals for each other. They combined for 73 completions, 1,250 yards, and 13 touchdowns during the 1991 season. The team had a 12-1 record. Cooper and Peyton had never felt closer to each other. "That year made us buddies," Cooper later said. Peyton agreed. "It's the most fun I ever had playing football," he said.

When Cooper graduated, he went to Ole Miss, as his father had. Peyton was sorry to see his brother leave home. He missed playing with him on their high school team. However, Cooper told Peyton not to worry. In two years, Peyton would graduate and go to Ole Miss too. Then the brothers would be teammates again.

A Change of Plans

Peyton Manning had the future all figured out. Cooper would be a star wide receiver at Ole Miss. Peyton would be a great quarterback at the school, just like his dad had been.

However, things did not work out quite the way the Manning family thought. A few months before his freshman year at Ole Miss, Cooper's right hand felt numb. Then his leg felt numb too. Archie and Olivia took him to see many doctors. Finally, they received terrible news. Cooper had an illness called spinal stenosis. This condition narrows the spinal cord. It can cause paralysis. Cooper had to have an operation. He could never play football again.

The Manning family was very upset by the news. Cooper worried about how Peyton would feel. He wrote Peyton a letter. It said, "I would like to live my dream of playing football through you. Although I cannot play anymore, I know I can still get the same feeling out of watching my little brother do what he does best."

Cooper's illness changed Peyton's feelings about football. Despite his parents' teachings, Peyton had always felt that

Peyton tries to complete a pass as he is grabbed from behind by Mike Moten of the Florida Gators.

playing football was the most important thing in life. Now he realized that family and good health were more important. "Cooper's condition taught me to appreciate life and to realize, hey, there's more to life than football," Peyton said. He also realized how quickly life could change. "Any play could be my last, so I try my best on every one," he said.

Peyton graduated from Isidore Newman in 1994. During his spectacular high school career, he had passed for more than 7,200 yards. He threw 92 touchdown passes. In three seasons, his team won 34 games and lost only 5. An organization called the Touchdown Club in Columbus, Ohio, named Peyton the best offensive high school player in the nation. Sports magazines, newspapers, and television shows talked about this star quarterback.

> *An organization called the Touchdown Club . . . named Peyton the best offensive high school player in the nation.*

Many colleges wanted Peyton to play for them after he graduated. He received hundreds of phone calls and letters from colleges all over the United States. He finally narrowed his choices down to two schools. One was Ole Miss. The other was the University of Tennessee.

For years, Peyton had been sure he would attend Ole Miss. However, Cooper's illness changed Peyton's mind. The dream of playing with his brother was over. Peyton did not want to go to a school where he would be a hero just because of who his father was.

It would have been easy for Archie to tell Peyton what to do. However, Archie did not. "All I told him was 'I'm here for you, but you make the call,'" he said.

Finally, Peyton made up his mind. He would attend the University of Tennessee in Knoxville. He would play for the school's football team, the Volunteers.

College Star

*P*eyton arrived at school six weeks early so that he could train with the other members of the team. He knew that he probably would not play much during his first season. Still, he wanted to be ready. He wanted to feel like part of the Volunteers.

Peyton's chance to play for Tennessee came sooner than anyone expected. During the team's first game, Tennessee's starting quarterback was injured. Another player replaced him, but he did not play well. The coach signaled Peyton to join the game.

Peyton quickly ran into the huddle and called a play. He moved the Volunteers a short distance down the field. Then he went back to the bench. He was disappointed that he did not get more time in the game. Still, he knew he would be on the field again soon.

Three weeks later, during the fourth game of the season, the Volunteers quarterback hurt his knee. Peyton went in the game to take over. The team lost the game, but Peyton played well. From then on, he was the Volunteers starting quarterback.

Peyton and the Volunteers had a good season. The team ended the year ranked 22 in the nation. Peyton was named the best freshman player in the Southeastern Conference.

Although football was Peyton's number one focus, he made time for other things, too. He was studying speech communication and business and got good grades. He was also dating another student, Ashley Thompson.

However, Peyton devoted most of his time to football. He knew hard work would make him a better player. He spent so much time in his room watching tapes of the Volunteers' games that his roommates called him Caveman.

Peyton's hard work paid off. The Volunteers lost only one game during the 1995 season. The team was ranked number three in the nation. Peyton set several team records.

His junior year brought more football glory. He became the first Tennessee quarterback to throw for more than 3,000 yards in a season. The team had a 10-2 record. Peyton received so much attention that he started wearing disguises whenever he went out.

Many people expected Peyton Manning to win the Heisman Trophy that year. This award is given to the best college football player in the nation. Manning was excited about the chance to win the Heisman. However, he was more interested in leading his team to a winning season. "I'm not about the Heisman," he said. "I'm about wins and losses." In the end, Peyton did not win the award.

During his junior year, Peyton had a big decision to make. Should he leave school to play in the NFL? Or should he stay in college for one more year? Some of the top college football stars do not stay in school for more than three years. NFL coaches were eager for Peyton to join the league. He would be the number-one choice in the NFL draft.

Peyton looks for an open receiver as he drops back for a pass during a game between the Tennessee Volunteers and the Kentucky Wildcats.

Peyton had already taken enough classes to graduate. He had a 3.61 grade point average. Also, he was healthy and strong. If he left for the NFL then, he could make a lot of money. If he played for Tennessee for one more year, he might be injured. If that happened, he might not be able to play in the NFL at all.

> **Finally, Peyton knew what he had to do. He told everyone he would be staying at the University of Tennessee. . . . Tennessee fans were thrilled.**

As he always did when he had a choice to make, Peyton took the time to think about things. He talked to his coaches. He talked to NFL players who had left school early to turn pro. Of course, he talked to his family, too.

Finally, Peyton knew what he had to do. He told everyone he would be staying at the University of Tennessee. "Believe me, I looked at the money," he said. "I'm hoping the money's there next year, too. But staying was the strongest thing in my heart. I wanted to come back and be a college student one more year."

Tennessee fans were thrilled at the news. As Peyton went back to his room, he saw thank-you banners hanging all over school. Tennessee's government was pleased too. They issued a statement, saying, "In this time of unbridled greed and diminished loyalty, it is indeed refreshing to see a young man honor his commitments to his school and his teammates. He represents everything that is admirable about our young people today."

Many NFL coaches agreed that Peyton had made a good decision. Bill Parcells was the coach of the New York Jets. That team would probably have drafted Peyton if he had turned pro. Parcells said, "I think the common feeling in this country today is that everybody sells out for the money and the opportunity. I admire Peyton's decision and think that it took courage to make it. I think it's refreshing, really."

Peyton had a wonderful time during his senior year of college. He led the Volunteers to an 11-1 season. The Volunteers played Nebraska for the national championship. Although Nebraska won, it was still a great achievement for the Volunteers to get that far.

Once again, Peyton was a favorite to win the Heisman Trophy. Once again, he did not get it. Peyton was not very upset. "I was never taught to play for individual awards," he said. However, he was pleased to receive the Sullivan Award in February 1998. This award is given to the nation's top amateur athlete in all sports. Manning told reporters, "It's really very humbling when a person is selected to receive an award for something he loves to do."

> *Manning told reporters, "It's really very humbling when a person is selected to receive an award for something he loves to do."*

Peyton took pleasure in his stellar college career. Later, he wrote, "When I look back on it now, no dollar amount could equal what that last year in Knoxville meant to me. I'll always be a Tennessee Volunteer for the rest of my life."

Peyton's college career was finally over. It was time for the NFL.

The Colts on the March

*T*he Indianapolis Colts chose Peyton first in the 1998 NFL draft. Manning became the highest-paid rookie in the history of the NFL. They gave him a six-year contract worth $48 million. The Colts also announced that he would be their starting quarterback. That was very unusual for a rookie.

Manning and the Colts got off to a rough start. They lost the first four games of the 1998 season. "I made some mistakes," Manning admitted after throwing three interceptions in one game. "Hopefully I'll learn from them."

He did learn. The Colts won their fifth game. However, the team struggled to a 3-13 record for the season. Manning called the season "frustrating and disappointing. But you can either sit there and feel sorry for yourself or learn from it and do something about it."

Even though his team did not have a winning record, Manning had a very good year. He had the best rookie season in NFL history. He also broke a record by throwing 26 touchdown passes. He soon earned the respect of his

Peyton Manning stands with his parents and brothers after being chosen by the Indianapolis Colts in the first round of the 1998 NFL draft.

teammates, too. "He's always working on something," said teammate Mark Thomas. "He's here early and stays late."

In 1999, the Colts were a different team. They beat almost every other team in the league and ended the season with a 13-3 record. No team in history had improved so much in just one year. Manning also set a new team record when he passed for 4,135 yards. Although the Colts lost in the playoffs, they knew they were finally a great team.

Manning led the Colts to another winning season in 2000. That year, he became only the fifth quarterback to pass for 4,000 yards in consecutive seasons. However, once again the Colts lost in the playoffs.

The 2001 season was not a good one for the Colts. At the end of the season, the head coach and his staff were all fired. The team would have to start over in 2002.

Luckily, 2002 turned out to be a good year for the Colts—and for Manning. Once again, the Colts made the playoffs, although they lost to the New York Jets. Manning also became the only player in NFL history to pass more than 4,000 yards four years in a row.

In 2003, the Colts finally won their first playoff game. After another winning season, they defeated the Denver Broncos. Then they defeated the Kansas City Chiefs. However, the New England Patriots defeated the Colts the following week. The Patriots went on to win the Super Bowl that year. Even though his team did not make the championship, Manning was named one of the NFL's Most Valuable Players.

Manning poses between Colts owner Jim Irsay (left) and Colts president Bill Polian with his 2003 MVP trophy.

He shared the honor with Steve McNair, the quarterback of the Tennessee Titans. Manning also played in the Pro Bowl, which is the NFL's all-star game.

The Colts were so pleased with Manning that they gave him a new contract in 2004. This time, he would be paid more than $99 million over seven years. Manning had another great season that year. The high point was when he threw his 49th touchdown pass. The pass broke football legend Dan Marino's record. Manning also broke Brett Favre's record when he

Manning holds his MVP trophy after the 2005 NFL Pro Bowl. He qualified for the Pro Bowl six times between 1999 and 2005.

Colts fans hold up a banner and celebrate after Manning beats Dan Marino's record for touchdown passes.

threw at least two touchdown passes in 13 straight games. "Amazing," Favre said. "The guy is a winner."

In October 2005, Manning threw his 86th touchdown pass to teammate Marvin Harrison. This broke the NFL record for a quarterback-receiver pair. In November, they broke the record for yardage gained by a pair: over 10,000.

Manning enjoyed setting records. However, he was even more pleased when his efforts helped his team win. In 2005, he told a reporter from *Football Digest*, "I feel I have to do my part — that for us to win, I have to play at a high level."

The Colts won 13 straight games that season. In January 2006, Manning led his team to the division playoffs. However, the Colts lost to the Pittsburgh Steelers.

Marvin Harrison (#88) is congratulated by Peyton Manning (#18) after they achieved the NFL record for touchdown passes on October 17, 2005.

Giving Back

Archie and Olivia Manning always taught their children that it was important to give back. As soon as he signed his first professional contract, Peyton started doing just that.

He started a charity called the PeyBack Foundation. The foundation raises money for children in need. One of the PeyBack Foundation's most popular events is a series of high school football games called the PeyBack Classic. The games are played in RCA Dome, the stadium where the Colts play. By 2006, they had raised about $120,000 for high schools in Indianapolis. Peyton has also donated thousands of dollars to food banks, the Boys and Girls Clubs, and Special Olympics.

In 2001, Peyton married Ashley Thompson. The two had been dating since Peyton's freshman year in college. Ashley works with him on his charitable activities. The couple especially enjoys helping children during the holidays. Their foundation has donated hundreds of thousands of dollars to Toys for Tots and the Christmas for Kids Campaign.

Peyton holds young Stanley Whatley at the Children's Hospital of Michigan after FedEx, an NFL sponsor, donated $25,000 to the hospital.

In August 2005, Peyton's hometown of New Orleans was devastated by Hurricane Katrina. The Mannings' home was not seriously damaged, but the family knew that many people in the area were not as lucky. Peyton got together with his younger brother, Eli, who is the quarterback of the New York Giants. Together they organized a plane full of 30,000 pounds of supplies. Then the brothers flew down to help people in the affected areas. The PeyBack Foundation also sold wristbands to raise money for hurricane relief.

Peyton holds his father up as an example for everything he does. "I get asked all the time why I give myself so freely," Peyton wrote. "Easy. I learned from the master. Those who look up to you for whatever reason ought to get something positive in return. It's the right thing to do, so do the right thing."

Peyton takes being a role model very seriously. He does not agree with athletes who do not accept their responsibilities. "I've tried to keep myself out of bad situations, and if that means I'm a Goody Two-shoes, so be it. I have a great opportunity here. Why not reach out and help someone be a good person, resist temptation, and stay in school? That's the person I want to be. My parents taught me to do the right thing, and that's what I try to do."

Peyton is proud of himself and his family. His family is proud of him. Other people are too. Bill Polian, the president of the Indianapolis Colts, once said, "When you think about all the good things that happen—good sportsmanship and preparation and commitment to a team and his teammates—we think about Peyton. He's everything that is good about sports."

CHRONOLOGY

1976 Peyton Manning is born in New Orleans, Louisiana, on March 24.

1991 Peyton becomes the starting quarterback for the Isidore Newman School.

1994 Peyton graduates from Isidore Newman; he is named the best offensive high school player in the nation; he attends the University of Tennessee and is named Southeastern Conference Freshman of the Year.

1998 Peyton wins the Sullivan Award; he graduates from University of Tennessee and is selected first in the NFL draft by the Indianapolis Colts; he starts his PeyBack Foundation.

1999 Peyton helps the Colts to a winning season; he plays in the Pro Bowl for the first time.

2000 Peyton becomes the fifth quarterback in NFL history to pass for over 4,000 yards in consecutive seasons.

2001 Peyton marries Ashley Thompson.

2003 Peyton leads the Colts to the playoffs; he is named NFL co-MVP.

2004 The Colts sign Peyton to a new contract.

2005 Peyton throws his 86th touchdown pass to teammate Marvin Harrison to break the NFL record for a quarterback-receiver pair.

2006 Peyton is named the 2005 Walter Payton NFL Man of the Year, which honors a player's community service as well as his football talent.

CAREER STATS

Year	Team	G	GS	Att	Comp	Pct	Yards	YPA	Lg	TD	Int	Rate
1998	Colts	16	16	575	326	56.7	3739	6.50	78	26	28	71.2
1999	Colts	16	16	533	331	62.1	4135	7.76	80	26	15	90.7
2000	Colts	16	16	571	357	62.5	4413	7.73	78	33	15	94.7
2001	Colts	16	16	547	343	62.7	4131	7.55	86	26	23	84.1
2002	Colts	16	16	591	392	66.3	4200	7.11	69	27	19	88.8
2003	Colts	16	16	566	379	67.0	4267	7.54	79	29	10	99.0
2004	Colts	16	16	497	336	67.6	4557	9.17	80	49	10	121.1
2005	Colts	16	16	453	305	67.3	3747	8.27	80	28	10	104.1
Total		**128**	**128**	**4333**	**2769**	**63.9**	**33189**	**7.66**	**86**	**244**	**130**	**93.5**

(G=Games, GS=Games started, Att=Attempts, Comp=Completions, Pct=Percentage, YPA=Yards per attempt, Lg=Longest pass, TD=Touchdown, Int=Interceptions)

FURTHER READING

For Young Readers

Bradley, Michael. *Peyton Manning*. New York: Benchmark Books, 2003.

Rappoport, Ken. *Super Sports Star Peyton Manning*. Berkeley Heights, NJ: Enslow Publishers, 2003.

"Rules for Everyone." *Scholastic News*, September 5, 2005, Vol. 62, Issue 1.

Savage, Jeff. *Peyton Manning: Precision Passer*. Minneapolis: Lerner Sports, 2001.

Stewart, Mark. *Peyton Manning: Rising Son*. Brookfield, CT: Millbrook Press, 2000.

Wilner, Barry. *Sports Great Peyton Manning*. Berkeley Heights, NJ: Enslow Publishers, 2003.

Works Consulted

Attner, Paul. "Player of the Year Peyton Manning COLTS." *Sporting News*, February 11, 2005, Vol. 229, Issue 6, p. 8.

Collie, Ashley Jude. "X's and O's." *Football Digest*, November 2005, Vol. 35, Issue 3, pp. 12–21.

Manning, Archie and Peyton. *Manning*. New York: Harper Entertainment, 2000.

Pedulla, Tom. "Colts Connection Makes History." *USA Today*, October 19, 2005.

Pompei, Dan. "Man, Oh, Manning." *Sporting News*, September 16, 2005, Vol. 229, Issue 37, pp. 14–22.

Wilner, Barry. "A Season for the Ages." *Football Digest*, Spring 2005, Vol. 34, Issue 7, pp. 24–30.

On the Internet

Indianapolis Colts
http://www.colts.com
NFL.com: Peyton Manning
http://www.nfl.com/players/playerpage/12531
Peyton Manning.com
http://www.peytonmanning.com
Peyton Manning Field
http://www.peytonmanning18.com

INDEX